Nature's Children

MUSKOX

Merebeth Switzer

GROLIER
EDUCATIONAL

FACTS IN BRIEF

Classification of the muskox
- Class: *Mammalia* (mammals)
- Order: *Artiodactyla* (cloven-hoofed mammals)
- Family: *Bovidae* (famly of antelopes, cattle, sheep and goats)
- Genus: *Ovibos*
- Species: *Ovibos moschatus*

World distribution.   Northern Canada, Alaska and Greenland; introduced in other Polar regions.

Habitat.   Arctic tundra.

Distinctive physical characteristics.   Completely covered in long dark hair, lighter in a patch on the back and "stockings;" long horns that grow down and out.

Habits.   Live in large herds; active during the day regardless of the availability of daylight.

Diet.   Weeds, shrubs and grasses.

Published originally as
"Getting to Know . . . Nature's Children."

This series is approved and recommended by the Federation of Ontario Naturalists.

Contents

Imagine visiting the Arctic in winter. Cold winds howl across the frozen tundra. Snow swirls all around. There is no sign of life. Or is there? Off in the distance are some huddled brown forms. What can they be?

They are muskoxen, gathered together to stay warm.

You have to be a pretty amazing animal to survive in a land where winter comes in September and stays until June. How can muskoxen stand the cold? Where do they find food in winter when snow blankets the ground?

Fortunately muskoxen are well-equipped for life in this frozen land.

Not an Ox at All

Do not be fooled by the muskox's name. It is not an ox at all. And it is not related to the bison either, though it looks rather like one. Instead, the muskox's closest relatives are goats.

Like goats, muskoxen are cud chewers. This means that they swallow their food whole, store it in a special part of their stomach and then bring it back to their mouth and chew it later. Muskoxen also have short goat-like tails, and they can climb like goats.

It is no mystery where the *musk* in the muskox's name came from. The male gives off a strong musky odor once a year when it is ready to mate.

But the muskox has another name that was given to it by the people who know it best. The Inuit call it Omingmak, meaning "the bearded one." One look at a muskox in its long, shaggy coat and you will see that this is a very good name.

The bearded one.

Living at the Ends of the Earth

Muskoxen once roamed all over the lands that surround the Arctic Ocean. They lived in Eurasia, Greenland, Alaska, mainland Canada and some of the Arctic Islands. But in the 1800s they were hunted for their meat and fur until they were nearly all gone.

Today muskoxen are protected. There are nearly 10 000 of them in northern Canada. They also occur naturally in Greenland and some have been taken to live in Iceland, the Soviet Union and Alaska.

Where muskoxen live in North America.

Even in summer, you would probably find Ellesmere Island beautiful but forbidding. To these muskoxen, it is home.

How Big?

In photographs, muskoxen often look enormous. But if you could visit them on the tundra, you would find that they are smaller than you might expect.

The shoulder hump of even a large adult male or bull would reach only to about your dad's chin. The muskox has a stocky body with short legs. The males can weigh from 200 to 400 kilograms (500 to 900 pounds). The females, or cows, weigh a little less than the bulls.

A bull's-eye view.

That Fantastic Fur Coat

Are you surprised to find that the muskox is not as big as you thought? Many people are fooled because the muskox's long, thick fur coat makes it look very big and bulky. Muskoxen probably have the longest hair of all wild animals, and they need it to keep them warm. Their coat also protects them from insects.

The hair is dark brown or almost black over most of the body, with a creamy to yellowish brown saddle-shaped marking on the back. The cows and young muskoxen have lighter hair on their foreheads.

The coat is curly at the shoulders, but hangs long and straight everywhere else. A muskox has especially thick, long hair at the front of its body. On windy winter days, it faces into the wind, so that this hair gets pressed tightly against its body, which helps keep in the heat.

Opposite page:

A super-thick coat has its uses even in summer. It protects the muskox from mosquitoes and flies.

Two Coats in One

What would you do if you had to face the freezing arctic winter without any shelter? First, you would make sure you had super-thick wool long-johns to put on under your outer clothing. Well, the muskox is admirably equipped in that department. Its fur coat is actually two coats in one.

The outer coat of long sleek guard hairs keeps out wind and blowing snow. Under this, grows a thick inner coat of soft fur. This warm, fine fleece completely covers the animal except for its lips and nostrils. Air warmed by the muskox's body gets trapped in this thick fleece.

And how would you keep your ears warm if you had to spend all winter out in the cold? Wear a hat? A muskox does not need a hat. Its ears are short and furry and fit closely to its body. They are almost impossible to see under its shaggy fur coat. The muskox's stubby tail is well hidden by warm fur too. Having small, furred ears and tail means the muskox loses less body heat through them.

Messy Shedder

In April or May the muskox starts to shed its fine inner coat. Gradually thick tufts of it work their way up through the heavy guard hairs.

If you saw a muskox at this time of year you might think it was sick. The fur hangs off the animal in big grayish brown clumps and makes the muskox look tattered and moth-eaten. Long pieces of fur blow in the wind. Some fur clumps stick to the rocks and bushes on which the muskoxen have rubbed themselves. But by mid-July the shedding is over, and the muskoxen have a new dark undercoat.

What happens to all the fur the muskoxen shed? Arctic birds use it to line their nests!

Changing clothes.

Keen Senses

Although the muskox's ears are almost buried in fur, it has a very keen sense of hearing.

You might also think that all that hair makes seeing difficult for the muskox but this is not the case. The muskox has excellent eyesight and can even see well in faint light. This is important because winter days on the tundra are very short and the nights are long. In the northernmost parts of the muskox's range, there may be no real daylight for weeks as the sun does not rise above the horizon.

As well, this shaggy wonder has a good sense of smell.

Too Heavy Means Too Hot

Imagine wearing a fur coat all summer long!
Whew! You would get very, very hot, right?
That is what happens to muskoxen in summer.
Although they like to run and play, they soon
become overheated because of their two
protective coats.

When you get hot you perspire through
millions of sweat glands that cover your body.
But in its whole body, a muskox has only two
sweat glands, located on its back feet. So the
muskox cannot cool off by perspiring, and it
gets hot and tired very quickly. It can only be
active for a little while and then it must rest. If
there are still mounds of snow around, a hot
muskox may try to cool down by lying in one.

A young muskox's coat is short and curly.

Home on the Tundra

Muskoxen do not have special feeding areas as many other animals do. They do not even have a home where they sleep each night. Instead, they roam over the arctic plains, stopping wherever they find food.

In the summertime they look for places where the plants are lush and green. River valleys that have been covered with rich soil after a spring flood make good summer range for muskoxen because lots of plants grow there.

In the wintertime, muskoxen move to higher ground. They look for ridges or hills where the wind has blown away the snow, exposing grass or low bushes. But there is little food available in the winter, and the muskoxen may have to roam very far to get enough to eat.

In summer, muskoxen roam coastal plains and river valleys where food is most abundant.

Summer Salads

What do muskoxen eat? In the summer they dine on grasses and plants such as willowherb, knotweed, fleabane and bladder campion. The fresh green leaves of tiny arctic trees make a tasty treat. Although the tundra is almost always defined as "treeless," several kinds of trees, such as willow, birch and alder, do grow there. But they grow very slowly and never very big. A tree that's a hundred years old may be no more than a metre (3 feet) tall— which puts its leaves at a perfect height for a muskox to munch on.

Believe it or not, the muskox has no upper front teeth. To eat it must grip the food between its tongue or lower teeth and the roof of its mouth.

Frozen Dinner

In winter there is a lot less food available for the muskoxen, and most of it is covered with snow. Their winter food is mainly crowberry, bilberry, Labrador tea and the small, stunted trees of the tundra.

Sometimes, when the snow forms a thick crust over everything, the muskox must dig for food. It uses its sharp hoofs to paw through the icy snow. If that does not work, the muskox will use its head. Yes, its head! It will break the ice layer on the snow by pounding its head through the crust. Then it uses its hoofs to push away the broken ice chunks and get to the food below.

These muskoxen will have to work hard to find food here.

Very Impressive Horns

The muskox has a huge head crowned by a large pair of horns. The horns turn upwards and outwards. The tips are worn and polished while the rest of the horns are ribbed and ridged.

You can easily tell the female muskox from the bull if you look at the horns. The cow's horns are smaller, and they are separated by a patch of fur on the forehead. The bull's horns are larger and are very broad at the base where they join the forehead. This wide band of horn and the thick bone underneath protect the muskox's skull.

The horns are pale colored on a young muskox and turn dark brown as the animal gets older. It takes about six years for a muskox's horns to grow to their full adult size.

The horns tell it all. This is a young bull muskox.

Handy Hoofs

Ice and snow can be difficult to walk on unless you have special footwear. The muskox does. Its hoofs have sharp rims and rough heel pads that give it good traction on slippery surfaces.

In winter, fur grows on the heel pads for even more traction. And the hoofs are wide enough to help spread the muskox's great weight out over the snow. This helps to keep it from sinking in.

A muskox also finds its hoofs handy for something other than getting around. The front ones are larger than the back ones, and they make good shovels when the muskox must dig through the snow for food.

Muskoxen climb rocky slopes with ease.

Good Company

Hoof prints

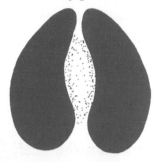

Front

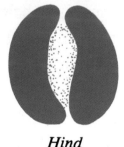

Hind

Muskoxen generally travel in groups, or herds. A muskox herd may contain anywhere from 3 to 100 animals, but the average is 15.

The herds may change in size from time to time. A large herd may break into several smaller ones. Or a number of small herds may join together to form one large one. Usually the herds will be larger in winter. Sometimes, the herds will be made up mostly of females and their young, with the bulls wandering about alone or in small bachelor groups. Other times they will be mixed, male and female, young and old.

The more the merrier!

A Wall of Muskoxen

Muskoxen have very few enemies. The wolf is their main predator and the Grizzly Bear may also attack them. When threatened, they protect themselves by forming a tight circle with the calves at the center. The adults stand with their horned heads pointing out.

Instead of just waiting for the predator to leave, one or more bulls may rush from the circle to attack. They take turns doing this so that none ever gets too tired. The bulls are extremely agile and can run surprisingly fast as they try to gore or trample their attacker.

When it is very cold the muskoxen form a triangle. The bulls hunch up their shoulders and face into the wind. The calves and cows form the other two sides of the triangle, protected from the wind by the bulls.

Overleaf:
Defense formation.

Within the muskoxen's range, temperature of -45° Celsius (-50° Fahrenheit) are common in winter.

A Walking Icicle

After a heavy snowfall or sleet storm a muskox often looks like a walking icicle. Melting ice or snow sometimes forms icicles which hang from the muskox's coat. The muskox cannot bite off the icicles. Instead it carries them around and they tinkle like bells as the muskox walks.

Huddled together against the cold.

Mating Time

The cows and bulls mate in September, but before this two males sometimes challenge each other for the right to mate with a cow. At this time, the male gives off the musky odor that gave the animal its name. The scent comes from a gland near the bull's eyes and he spreads it over his front legs by rubbing them with his head.

In late summer the tundra resounds with the noise of battling males. The challengers charge at each other and meet head-on with a deafening crash. Fortunately most of the force of the crash is absorbed by the muskox's thick horns and skull.

The bulls continue to charge at each other until one finally loses courage and veers off at the last minute. If neither backs off, the bulls continue to fight with head-to-head pushing, hooking of horns and wrestling until one is so exhausted he gives up.

Two heavy-weights square off.

Tundra Baby

The baby muskox is born in late April or early May, about eight months after the adults mate. This is still mid-winter in the Arctic, but the babies have to be born this early to allow them lots of time to grow up before next winter. Usually there is just one baby but some mothers have twins.

A newborn calf weighs about nine kilograms (20 pounds) which is about the weight of an adult raccoon. The baby begins to drink its mother's milk almost immediately. It gathers strength rapidly and is able to stand within minutes. In a few hours, it is strong enough to keep up with the herd.

"I'm the King of the Castle!"

Mother and Baby

The muskox is born with a short, curly dark brown coat. It does not grow long guard hairs like its parents until its third winter. Until then it must stick close to its mother and snuggle up to her warm side.

The mother only gives birth every other year and so she has lots of time to look after her baby. And what a fast growing baby! It begins nibbling tender grass shoots within a week of being born but continues to nurse on its mother's rich milk for over a year. By the time the calf is one year old it weighs 90 kilograms (200 pounds)—10 times what it weighed when it was born.

Although the young muskox is born with no horns at all, small bumps sprout on its forehead when it is about six months old. By the time it is a year old, the horns are six centimetres (2.5 inches) long, and at age two they are almost three times that long.

Fun and games.

Growing Up

The young calves like playing and racing about. They love to butt one another, and their favorite game is King of the Castle. One clambers to the top of a mound and paws the ground, challenging anyone to knock it off. Since it is just a game, no one gets hurt. Soon there is a new King of the Castle, and a new round of butting starts.

Butting games prepare the calves for battles when they are older, either with other muskoxen or against their enemies. The calves must grow up quickly in their arctic home. With the help of the rest of the herd they can live to be 20 years old and have several babies of their own.

Words to Know

Bull   Male muskox.

Calf   Young muskox.

Cow   Female muskox.

Cud   Hastily swallowed food brought back for chewing by cud chewers such as cows, deer and muskoxen.

Fleece   The woolly inner layer of a muskox's coat.

Guard hairs   Long coarse hairs that make up the outer layer of the muskox's coat.

Hoofs   Feet of deer, goats, muskoxen and some other animals.

Mate   To come together to produce young.

Nurse   To drink milk from a mother's body.

Predator   Animal that hunts other animals for food.

Tundra   Vast northern plains.

INDEX

Cover Photo: Stephen J. Krasemann (Valan Photos)
Photo Credits: R. Harrington (Miller Services), page 4; Stephen J. Krasemann (Valan Photos), pages 7, 15, 16, 19, 20, 23, 29, 33, 40; Norman Lightfoot (Eco-Art Productions), pages 8, 12, 24; J.D. Taylor (Miller Services), page 11; Mike Beedele (Miller Services), page 26; Fred Bruemmer, pages 30, 34, 36-37, 38, 42, 45.

Printed and Bound in Italy by Lego SpA